Cont

Foreword, by Stan Utley

Introduction: What Kind of Player do You Want to Be?

1: The Science and Art of Improvement

2: Your First Scoring Lesson

3: Goal-Setting and Benchmarking

4: Playing Lesson Formats and Strategies

Bonus: The Next Step

Acknowledgements

Foreword

By Stan Utley

I **met Joe Bosco for the first time years** ago when he came out to see me at Grayhawk Golf Club in Arizona for a day of lessons. He and his teaching partner were checking out what I had to say about putting and the short game to see if it would work for some of the clinics they were giving in Chicago. It was the start of a great relationship. I've spent quite a few days sharing my thoughts alongside Joe at the Glen Club. He's a good friend and an excellent teacher, and you can't help but respect the impact Joe has had with his students—especially his success with junior players.

When he described the concept of playing your own three-ball scramble, I could immediately see how it would be a great way for a player to find more confidence on the course. It's something I incorporated into my own practice routine this season as I got ready for Champions Tour golf, and I even used it to help my daughter get started in the game. By going into each shot with more than one chance to hit a good one, it took the pressure off—and it showed her that the ability to eventually make a good score was in her.

And that's really the key lesson in Real Golf. You might be a 100-shooter—or 90-shooter or an 80-shooter—right now. But you already have the skills to be a few shots better than that. You just need to have the confidence and freedom to see it, and to know how to break that barrier. There's no shortcut around actually learning the game's most important skills, but Joe's program shows you what kind of score you can shoot if you make good decisions and play your own best game with the skills you already have. It's a great way to think about golf, and I know it can help you if you give it a try.

Stan Utley
PGA Tour winner
and Golf Digest 50 Best Teacher

Scottsdale, AZ
November 19, 2013

Introduction

What Kind of Player Do You Want to Be?

"Every experience is mental, therefore every physical experience is ultimately a mental one."

Every player has beaten balls **on** the driving range working on his or her game, either alone or with a teacher. Everyone has paged through a copy of Golf Digest looking for the latest tip, or watched an instructional video looking for the easiest way to lower scores.

But all of that access to top-tier instruction, video swing analysis and game improving equipment hasn't made golfers any better as a group. The average handicap index hasn't budged in 30 years. It's still the same 19.1.

Why?

Because instruction is delivered inefficiently—even if it appears to be ideally suited to the player.

I've spent 25 years learning from and working with the best teachers in the country—people like Mike Adams, Stan Utley and Hank Haney. I've also been fortunate enough to be nominated for Golf Magazine's Top 100 list each of the last two iterations. I also know that your city, county or state is undoubtedly filled with golf instructors with training in how the golf swing works and reasonable ability to share ideas on technique.

So what makes me different? Why should you listen to what I have to say?

Because I'm one of the few teachers who has been able to adapt and organize the techniques management consultants, NBA coaches, the Marine Corps and Harvard Business School have been using to produce elite performers for years. Tiger Woods' first teacher, Rudy Duran, intuitively used some of these techniques to help Tiger develop his playing skills as a kid.

Before you start wondering if you have to be an elite athlete or a genius to be able to use this information, I can tell you from 25 years sharing these techniques that they work for any player—from aspiring tour professional to everyday amateur.

Anyone can improve in a much more direct and enjoyable way using these time-tested and results-proven methods—which are backed by cutting-edge science and brain research.

Let me show you how.

Part of the reason I've been able to approach golf instruction from a different perspective is because I came to teaching on a different path than many other instructors.

I was born and raised in the suburbs of Chicago—first on the South Side, in Oak Lawn, and then on the North Side in Winnetka. I still live in Winnetka today, two miles from the house I grew up in.

My early introduction to the game wasn't so uncommon. I had some cousins, the Jigantis, in Winnetka—three boys—and they spent a lot of that first summer at the local park district golf course. I was seven years old, bigger than average, and I fancied myself as a bit of an athlete. I scoffed at the idea of playing golf, but the youngest of my cousins, Paul Jiganti, dragged me over to the local par-3 course because we didn't have anything better to do.

On the 8th hole, I skulled one over the water with a 7-iron and ended up a foot from the hole. I made my first birdie, and I was hooked.

That summer, I shagged balls for the pro at the Winnetka Golf Club, and every summer from then through college and on to the point where I was able to open my first academy as an instructor, I worked at that same place.

I went to New Trier High School—which has played its home matches for years at Winnetka G.C.—and I was captain of the golf team my senior year, in 1982. I won the club championship there in 1988, the year before I decided to become a golf instructor.

My golf career stalled during my time at the University of Illinois. I wasn't quite good enough to make the team. I graduated with degrees in history and communications, and I figured I'd make my way in the business world.

Like a lot of Midwestern kids, after college, I made my way to downtown Chicago, where I got a job leasing office space. The golf boom was in full swing at the time—1987 and 1988—and I was working hard on my game and playing every weekend. The head pro at Winnetka Golf Club, Peter Donahue, was a great mentor of mine, and he and I started to knock around an idea that combined our two areas of expertise and passion. We'd build an indoor golf academy downtown, where businesspeople could take lessons on their lunch breaks or before or after work hours. We'd call it Loop Links, and it would make a mint.

We started raising money from investors with the thought of stocking the academy with the latest cutting edge simulators, so players could work on their games through the long Chicago winters. We were actually doing pretty well with the fundraising when I ended up in a meeting that would change my life.

A father of a girl I was dating at the time was an extremely successful businessman who had just retired from a long career at the consulting firm Coopers & Lybrand. His name was Raymond Tasch. Ray was gracious enough to agree to see me. Thanks to some nasty traffic I was late to our meeting, and he immediately let me have it. So I was pretty nervous when I gave him my elevator pitch about Loop Links.

It was the beginning of a mentoring relationship that lasted until Ray passed away in 2010. He had fought in World War II and cut his teeth at General Electric before moving on to C&L, where he performed outside evaluations for corporations that were looking to restructure.

I introduced Ray to Peter, and he sat us down and told his that he thought we had a great idea and the passion to make it work—but that we needed somebody with business experience to help make it work.

I was a sponge with both Ray and Peter. Peter taught me how to be a teacher, and Ray showed me how the elite businesses of the world run. Ray promised me he would teach me everything he knew about the consulting world—how to get people to think and learn along with you so that they can do what they do better. Ray called his approach "Dealing With Minds," and he pushed me to understand a process called POIM & A—Plan, Organize, Integrate, Measure & Adjust.

Ray had us tear up our original plan for the downtown academy and refund the money we had received from investors up to that point. Our new goal was to research the way the mind actually works and build a unique teaching program around those philosophies. The ideas we had—using sound and rhythm to teach the golf swing—are pretty mainstream now, but they were unheard of in the early 1990s.

Peter and I had a tremendous amount of success with our program—Rhythmic Golf. From the beginning, I was intent on helping my students take what we gave them in terms of mechanics and put them in a position where they could use it for real, on the golf course. I began walking the course with my students as they played, and helped them measure what their tendencies were under real game situations.

The results began to speak for themselves. My success with students of all ages and ability levels began to distinguish me from other teachers both in my academy and outside of it.

Players started making significant gains—when they had barely spent any time on the practice range. One player went from a 19 handicap to a 2 over the course of one summer. From day one, high school boys and girls players who aspired to make the strong New Trier High teams were on my schedule. They were soon joined by many fine junior players across the Chicagoland area—and that group was the first to go through the complete, early version of the program you're going to see here. One of those players ended up getting a scholarship to play for the University of Michigan, and she was followed up by another who would be a Rolex All-American and get a full ride to Northwestern.

The New Trier High School girls' team would go on to win four consecutive state championships from 2000-2003, and I taught six to eight players on each of those teams. I've had equal success with players on the boys' team—I've personally taught five individual state high school champions in the state of Illinois. In 2010, I began coaching the teams at the North Shore Country Day School (NSCD), right down the street from New Trier High. In the last four seasons, the NSCD boys' team has won two state championships and finished as runner up another time. My work with juniors gets most of the attention, but I've had just as much success with adult players. More than 50 of my adult students have won club championships across Chicagoland in the last 10 years.

My students and I were laboratory animals for my self-scrimmaging approach, but it was clear that we had found something unique. For years, players had been expected to go take lessons at the range, under controlled conditions, and then try to apply those lessons under different conditions—and under pressure. It didn't take much examination of the teaching techniques used by elite instructors in other disciplines—like the piano or fitness—to see that the traditional golf approach didn't work.

To be a virtuoso piano player, you have to actually play the piano. To win football games, you have to scrimmage.

As I built my teaching business, I called what I was doing a Consultative Approach. I didn't book students for the traditional single hour lesson or group of one or two lessons. My students would come for a morning and we'd go out and play the golf course for two or three hours—learning by doing. The fortunate side effect of my students' continuing success is that it has helped potential students come with an open mind and a willingness to discover what really matters in the game—not just a temporary tip or band-aid.

One of the central concepts I learned from Ray—who would go on to become my father-in-law when I married his lovely daughter Mary—is to always consider what happens when we think. Every experience is mental, therefore every physical experience is ultimately a mental one.

I could see that a vast majority of players gave virtually no thought to the mental part of the game, so I came up with two goals for myself. I wanted to learn as much as I could about how the mind works, and I wanted to be a rare teacher who delivered that mental component most effectively, so students could shoot their lowest scores ever.

If that sounds like something you want for your own game, turn the page.

CHAPTER 1

The Science and Art of Improvement

"Why is it such a challenge to take it to the course?"

When I took my earliest **steps** into teaching this game 25 years ago, I was struck by two of the most persistent questions students had. It seemed like every lesson began with one of two complaints—or both. Why, they asked, did it seem like lessons would offer some short-term benefits, but their handicap number never seemed to move much? And if they do lock onto something really helpful on the practice range, why is it such a challenge to take it out onto the course?

I'm certainly not the first teacher to hear these familiar complaints from students. And I'm not here to say that there aren't other teachers who have come up with ways to address these problems.

But I came to golf instruction from a different path than most teachers. My mentors have always encouraged me to look for inspiration and applicable solutions wherever I can find them—whether that's in a popular psychology bestseller, a breakdown of how elite Navy SEALs train, or first-hand description of the techniques used to incubate arguably the greatest golfer the game has ever seen.

There's no question I've been fortunate to know extremely talented mentors and teachers from a variety of disciplines throughout my career. Golf geniuses like Mike Adams, Hank Haney and Stan Utley have been generous with their time and insights on the game and how to teach it.

One mentor who has had a profound influence on my teaching style is someone everybody should know but not many do. Rudy Duran is a soft-spoken, modest, dedicated teaching professional from Southern California. He was the first instructor entrusted to work with Tiger Woods—when Tiger was four years old.

Rudy was obviously instrumental in helping reveal and develop the once-in-a-generation talent Tiger has—and he has a fantastic track record teaching hundreds of competitive adults and junior players throughout California. Part of my responsibility as a coach is to constantly improve my knowledge base and skills—and who could be a better mentor to me on the art of teaching serious players than the man who taught arguably the greatest of all time?

Rudy was generous enough to come to Chicago and teach schools with me that were geared toward parents and children. We had a wonderful time, and we went on to teach together at other clinics geared toward adult players—including one for Accenture at The Glen Club, my home base in Glenview, IL.

One night at dinner, Rudy was sharing some stories about the process he used with Tiger and Earl Woods. At the end of the meal, I asked him what he thought was the single most effective way to help players shoot lower scores.

His answer was very simple, and it became validation and foundation for my own teaching strategy—and the jumping off point for organizing the concepts in Real Golf.

Rudy's advice?

Play a self-scramble with three balls. At its core, it's a simple concept, but it has massive implications. After just nine holes keeping your three-ball ringer score, you get an immediate sense of your potential—with the skill set and swing you already have.

The next day, Rudy and I went out to the course and played just a few holes using this scramble technique. I immediately realized it was something I needed to develop for my own students.

Real Golf was born.

Rudy's final point about the self-scramble procedure—that it's hard to get players to actually go out and do it—was accurate. To make Real Golf really effective, I needed to understand why the scramble technique works as well as it does and how to get average players to see those benefits and consistently incorporate them into their own games. I needed to be able to coach it.

Most straightforward golf instruction—and golf psychology—just scratches the surface the core principles of brain function and human performance. But the reality is that playing golf isn't any different than playing tennis or a musical instrument or rappelling down a rock face in the middle of the night on a top-secret mission. All of those things require the mastery of a variety of complex skills, and the appropriate mental processing to apply those skills at the right time and in the right amounts. That means there's an entire world of information out there that isn't golf specific but can still be a tremendous help to those of us teaching and playing the game.

The concepts I learned from three people—Daniel Coyle, Dr. Sian Beilock and Dr. James Payne—have shaped the performance of thousands of high-achieving musicians, athletes and businesspeople, and have strongly influenced me as I develop and deliver Real Golf.

Daniel Coyle's work in the New York Times best-selling *The Talent Code* is probably the most familiar to the average reader. A researcher and contributing editor to Outside magazine, Coyle has studied and written about talent and achievement for more than a decade.

For *The Talent Code*, Coyle traveled around the world to visit "talent hotbeds"—small places that produced a disproportionate number of high achievers in a given discipline. He then reverse-engineered what those hotbeds did to develop talent to provide a blueprint for readers to develop their own.

The "success pattern" he describes in the book uses the brain's natural skill-acquisition mechanisms in the most efficient ways. The three key elements of that pattern are—in his lingo—ignition, master coaching and deep practice. The terminology doesn't matter as much as the theories themselves, and they certainly resonated with me.

Ignition is the overriding motivational factor a person brings to the table when trying to acquire a skill. If you have a commitment and a desire to learn something, you're going to be in a more receptive position to do so than if you're going through the motions.

Master coaching is the most straightforward—and in some ways, the trickiest—of the elements. The high achievers in the talent hotbeds Coyle studied had access to mentors who possessed very specific teacher traits. They helped the learners lay out specific performance benchmarks, they taught learners how to recognize and analyze feedback, and they gave them tools to evaluate and improve on their own as "self-coaches." I say that this element is tricky, because it's obviously a huge advantage to be one of the learners who happens to have access to master coaching. That hasn't been the reality for many golfers over their playing lives, but it's something I want to rectify with this Real Golf program.

The last element is the concept of deep practice. It bypasses rote, mechanical repetition for extremely focused situational recreations. The best example is one Coyle uses in the follow-up to *The Talent Code, the Little Book of Talent*. He describes the way Navy SEALS train for the infinite variety of dangerous missions they will undertake. Instead of repeatedly practicing specific rote elements, like low-altitude parachuting, marksmanship or building penetration, they run through incredibly realistic mission simulations that force them to make decisions and use skills on the fly. Not only are they practicing the discrete skills themselves, but they're practicing the framework in which all the skills work together. By the time they go on a real mission, the SEAL teams are confident that nothing they see will be a surprise.

Deep practice as a concept is perfect for the world of golf and golf instruction. Instead of hitting hundreds of balls on the range in an effort to perfect the ideal swing, deep practice involves going onto the golf course with an open attitude of information gathering. You're examining what you actually do in game situations, recording the results and using that feedback to guide your improvement.

That linkage between the self-scramble concept and deep practice is the key to Real Golf.

Dr. Sian Beilock has the rare gift of being able to make hard science extremely approachable for the casual reader. Nowhere is this more evident than in Choke, her entertaining book about the brain science behind performing under stress. Dr. Beilock has studied hundreds of athletes, from the elite level to the weekender—to better understand how people both acquire skills and seem to "forget" them when the game is on the line. Her work also expands into the world of music and business, where "choking" is an equally familiar term.

Dr. Beilock's book is great because it not only explains the "whys" of performance anxiety, but also provides proven techniques to overcome these problems. One the simplest ones involves writing out a basic paragraph about your fears and worries just before you play. By putting your feelings into words, you're changing how your brain deals with stressful situations. Instead of conjuring worst case scenarios, your brain gets to work subconsciously looking for solutions—which manifest themselves as clean performances of skills you already possess.

Another fantastic trick any player can use to beat on-course stress is the use of a "meditation." Everyone from Michael Jordan and Tiger Woods in sports to the CEOS of Goldman Sachs and Ford in business have talked about finding significant benefit in deep-focus meditation right before entering a stressful environment. I have developed a half-dozen specific meditation routines for my students that we'll talk more about in Chapter 4.

My good friend Dr. Jim Payne is a tenured professor of special education at the University of Mississippi, where he is an expert on how people think. For more than 30 years, he has researched the ways the mind produces certain behaviors—and how people in various disciplines can use their mind more productively. I found his book PeopleWise Putting: Getting Your Brain in the Game in a bookstore and was drawn to it. It illustrates how players can use the brain technology built into all of us to generate "Olympian focus" and build confidence. I reached out to Jim to learn more about his techniques and hopefully incorporate the most useful bits in ways that would help my students.

He came to Chicago for a visit, and we hit it off immediately. Jim and I developed a way to share a technique we call "pre-living"— where you use your imagination, emotion and visualization to vividly picture a scenario or a shot in its entirety before you actually do it in real life.

As I started to digest all of this expertise, I began to experiment with the foundation Rudy suggested. Using some of my most trusted students as "guinea pigs," I began to assign them some different kinds of homework. I asked them to try different simple variations of the three-ball personal scramble Rudy had described.

In a matter of months, it became very clear that playing lesson formats like the personal scramble—anchored in the hard science and practical brain technology expertise from folks like my friend Dr. Payne—were making a dramatic difference in my students' scores. Whether it was high school players morphing from mid-80s shooters to league champions or B-flight club players contending for their club championship, Real Golf was proving to be the real deal. By 2010, it became the core of all the lessons I taught.

Here is an actual email one of my students sent me after he tried the most basic version of the three-ball scramble for the first time, over 18 holes. Up to this point, he was a 14-handicap player who hadn't seen much improvement in more than a decade of taking lessons from conventional teachers.

Score	66
Fairways	10
Greens in regulation	15
Putts	27

1. I added up the total feet of putts I made and I'd guess it was around 105 feet. My birdie putts were on 2 (40'), 8 (20'), 10 (10'), 14 (on in 2 and 2 putted), 16 (20') and 18 (5'). The longest par putt I had to make was about 6'.

2. **Making some long putts and having only 27 putts is a huge stroke saver.** There was some luck in making three long putts, even with three tries. But I had birdie putts on 15 holes, so I definitely increased the odds of making some.

3. I think at the level I play the key to a good round, even a great round, is just not making mistakes. Having 3 tries at each shot allowed me to avoid any big mistakes. I had no penalties, no 3 putts, and even though I missed 4 fairways, I was on the green in regulation on 15 holes and close on the other three. I chipped well and only had to make one decent length putt to save par.

4. **Having 3 tries to make a shot takes a lot of pressure off and I think I swung more freely and was more relaxed in general. Interestingly, although I did not keep track, I would bet I used my first shot more often than my second or third.**

5. In general, I have felt I've been hitting the ball better lately but have to **learn to trust the swing changes I'm making.** I haven't put together a good, complete round yet but I know I'm close. I've had rounds where I've parred 3 and 7, but then had doubles on 14 and 15. That shouldn't happen. Obviously I avoided that where I had 3 tries to make the shot.

6. **Getting to see how a putt breaks certainly helps in trying to make it. (Building Visualization Experience!)**

7. I do think if I did this again I probably would not have as low a score as I did. I made some long putts and really was hitting the ball well. However, **I think I should always be able to be at par or even a little lower on a consistent basis. Again, the key is that this approach takes away most mistakes, and certainly all big mistakes.**

8. I think **this exercise shows the potential I have. Not necessarily for a 66, but certainly lower than my current handicap. I did not make many shots that were phenomenal. I did hit a lot of good, solid, quality shots.** My goal has to be to produce that on a more regular basis when I have one try at each shot. Again, the key is staying away from mistakes, especially big ones. I think if I just had no penalties or 3 putts ever, I'd average around 80, maybe better. This exercise eliminated those, plus gave me the chance to hit some good shots and make some putts.

This player, a man in his 50s, used to have trouble breaking 90. Now he frequently shoots rounds in the 70s. It doesn't matter if you're a 14-handicapper like this student, an aspiring college or professional player or a player who is relatively new to the game. You can use this method to get better by this weekend. To get started on your own Real Golf program, turn the page. I'll take you through it step-by-step.

NOTES

CHAPTER 2

Your First Scoring Lesson

"The best way to play better golf is to actually play golf."

Nothing is more seductive **than** the idea of a quick fix.

Admit it. You've seen the advertisements for the new $450 drivers and the promises of 30 more yards with the swipe of a credit card, and you've been tempted. You've paged through the latest issue of Golf Digest with hope that a tip from one of the teachers or players might change your game.

Now, we all know it isn't quite that simple. Real change doesn't come with a snap of the fingers. It will take some work to get better. Anybody who promises you anything different is setting you up for disappointment.

But the good news is that the classic formula for improving your game—hundreds of hours on the range and lesson after lesson with a pro—is obsolete. By focusing your effort on *playing* the game instead of just *swinging* the club, you will improve more quickly and shoot more satisfying scores.

You're going to start that today by taking your first Real Golf playing lesson.

My lesson book doesn't look like any other teacher's. Many of my students start the same way—with the diagnostic scoring lesson I'll describe in this chapter. I start my students with a comprehensive questionnaire that lets them self-assess where they think they are with their game. This process will not only give you a starting point for identifying those stress points we just discussed, but also reveal either hidden issues in your game or bust some misconceptions. For example, you might think of yourself as a terrible putter, but after the self-scramble and some extra chances to hit short game shots, you might see that your putting is actually pretty good when you aren't leaving yourself with 40-foot first putts all of the time!

The day before you go out to play your first self scramble, answer the following questions. (Or enter your answers and save them to your profile on RealGolfBook.com)

1. What was your best career round, and why? Was it purely because of score, or because of the toughness of the course or who your partners or opponents were?

2. Can you mentally replay that great round in your head? Shot by shot? Hole for hole? Which shots or holes are the most vivid?

3. What was your last bad round?

4. Can you mentally replay that round in your head? Which shots or holes are the most vivid?

5. What is your average nine-hole score?

6. What is your USGA handicap?

7. Using a 1-10 scale, how would you rate yourself in the following areas?

    a. Drives

    b. Fairway metals

    c. Hybrids

    d. Long/mid irons

    e. Short irons

    f. Full pitches with the SW and PW

    g. Pitching and chipping in short game

    h. Bunker

i. Putting

j. Course management

k. Practice effectiveness

l. Temperament

m. Trouble shots

n. Mental game

o. Belief in abilities

p. Equipment

8. What are two skills you WANT to improve?

9. What are two skills you NEED to improve?

10. Ask your playing partner to give you an honest assessment of your game. Does he or she think you played at approximately your handicap level? Above it? Below it?

Once you've completed the survey, you're ready to hit the course. And after nine holes where you play your best of three attempts on every shot, you'll have an intimate understanding of where your comfort zone and pressure points are. And better yet, you'll see how the actual process of *playing* will improve your results.

Does that mean you'll never have to hit another range ball again? Of course not. The range is still a great place to warm up before a round, blow off some steam at the end of the day, or to go and work on specific mechanical problems with your swing instructor.

But you'll quickly see why Real Golf is so much more effective than rote copying of swing positions or drills next to a giant bucket of balls on the range. The best way to play better golf is to actually play golf. So much more goes into a shot on the golf course—from decision making to mental preparation and risk analysis.

I don't want to make this sound like you're learning a completely new sport. Let me take you through the first scoring lesson step-by-step, so you can see just how close you are to discovering a better way to play.

At the start, don't change anything. Set up a time in the next week for a nine-hole practice round with a friend or two. When you get to the course, go through your normal pre-round routine—as you would for any other day. If that means hitting a bucket of balls beforehand and doing a series of stretches, go for it. If it means sitting on the patio and drinking a beer, by all means do it.

Once you've made it to the first tee, we're going to start doing a few things differently.

Open a new sleeve of balls, and use a Sharpie to mark each one with a number—1, 2 and 3. You're going to play this round essentially as a self-scramble, hitting three shots, picking the best result, then playing the next shot from that spot. The numbers on the balls are going to help you remember—and note on your card—which shot in the sequence you hit the best and worst. If you happen to lose one of the balls during the nine holes, replace it with one marked with the same number.

The concept of playing a "self-scramble" seems simple, but the effect it can have on your overall game is profound. One of the major roadblocks every player faces—whether he or she is on the professional tour or just trying to break 100 for the first time—is the ability to play one shot at a time. It's natural to look ahead and get anxious—or look back and stay angry about something you just did. The self scramble process helps you compartmentalize each "shot" into one element. For the purpose of this game, that element is three swings at three different balls. Once you've completed the process for those three swings—and completed the "shot"— you move onto the best one. The next sequence of balls constitutes the next shot.

At its most basic, the self scramble extends the time frame of one shot, both in time and the number of swings you get to complete it. You've got more time to concentrate on what happens during the shot. You can evaluate what happens with each swing—what went wrong and right. It's like getting two serves in tennis, or two free throws in basketball.

We've put training wheels on the shot process.

By extending each "shot" to three swings, you're also reducing one of the other main risks to your score—the downward spiral many players get sucked into after a bad mistake.

It's happened to all of us. You get to an important part of the round, when you really *need* to hit the fairway, and you get tight and snap hook one out of bounds. Or you fat yet *another* pitch shot. That bad shot carries over to the next one, and 20 minutes later you're looking down at consecutive doubles or triples on your card. And it becomes just another bad day on the course.

As you play the first hole—and the other eight afterward—hit the three shots in each sequence in what I call "awareness mode." Be objective and analytical about what happens on each one. I think of it as almost a clinical process, where I'm detached from what's going on. You want to measure the result of each shot—without the pressure of consequences—so you can build a storehouse of information on your game. You're taking the emotion out of it— staying out of "judgmental mode"—which helps you avoid either overstating or underestimating the issues you might have with your game.

Some questions you want to ask yourself after each swing are pretty straightforward:

-Can I hit the next one better?

-Can I duplicate what I just did?

-Can I correct what just happened?

-What caused that shot?

The answers to those questions are incredibly valuable—as long as you stay calm and objective. It's more useful to know how and why you hit your third tee shot better than your first on each hole vs. telling yourself how much you stink, or how you're never going to hit a good shot! The fact that you're approaching this through the lens of a nine-hole practice round—and not the final match of your club championship—should help you stay in this observational and not judgmental mindset.

The first time you hit what you might consider a perfect first or second shot—one you just can't see improving upon—resist the urge to skip the remaining swings in the sequence. Every swing in the exercise is a valuable chance to pick up information on your tendencies. What happens when the pressure to hit a good shot is off? Do you hit the next one better? Worse? What happens when you try a different swing thought or technique within the context of a real golf hole?

To score your personal scramble, print out one of the customizable scorecards from RealGolfBook.com, which has spaces to record the result of each swing you make for your nine holes. After you make the three swings for your tee shot, pick the best result of the three, then play the next series of swings from that spot. Continue through the nine holes using that same pattern. You'll make three swings for every "shot," and you'll be recording a ringer score for each hole—a composite result of the best swing from each "shot."

When you've finished nine holes, you're going to have a storehouse of information about your swing. You're also going to have what will most likely be a very encouraging barometer of your game's potential. That scramble score is a composite of shots you actually hit. If you normally shoot 41 or 42, and end up shooting 34 in the self-scramble format, you're showing yourself that you can hit the shots required to get under par for nine holes using one ball in time. That's an exhilarating feeling, and I've seen it on the faces of hundreds of my students.

If you have the time and inclination to try this exercise over 18 holes, you're welcome to give it a go, but I prefer the nine-hole variety in the beginning for a variety of reasons. You're making three full swings for every shot, which can take some time—and nine holes keeps the exercise within a manageable time slot. I'd rather have you sustain your focus intensely over two hours than have mediocre focus for four. It also gets you out of thinking about your score in terms of an 18-hole medal situation. For this exercise, a number like 79 or 89 or 102 isn't as important as what you're learning about your game—although I bet you'll be very surprised at your personal scramble score.

I've been using this technique with my students for almost 10 years, and I've had some express some reluctance about it at first. They usually say they don't have time to do it, or that they don't think it will prove anything. But I've never had a student come back from trying it and saying it didn't work, or that it didn't get them thinking about their game in a different way.

The key is to maintain your concentration and thought throughout the exercise. Machine-gunning ball after ball mindlessly out onto the range doesn't prove anything, and it won't help your game. The same concept applies here as well. If you do happen to go out and hit a series of bad shots right off the bat and get frustrated, I don't want you to lose interest and just mark time until the nine holes are finished. If you just aren't feeling it after a hole or two, go back in, take a few minutes and go hit some balls at the range. Try again at a different time. But the key is to get to a place mentally and emotionally where you treat this as an experiment, and are intrigued and interested by the results—not caught up in the ego of the score.

After you've finished your first personal scramble, you're ready to start pinpointing the real weaknesses in your game and building an on-course practice round routine that will help address those weaknesses.

Here are some key questions to ask yourself while the Real Golf self-scramble is still fresh in your mind:

1. What did you feel during the round?

2. If you were to track how often you used the first, second or third ball, what would you say?

3. What did you learn from the first shot?

4. Where you able to trend your shots in the right direction?

5. Did your tee shots improve?

6. Did your score improve as you went later in the round?

7. Did you learn about reading greens?

8. What types of shots gave you the most trouble?

9. Did your trouble areas continue to give you problems when you had more chances? If not, it could indicate more of a tension issue than a mechanical one.

10. What surprised you about the experience?

11. Was it more fun than you expected?

12. Any part of it that turned you off?

13. Knowing you had three chances, did you change your strategic approach compared to what you would have done normally?

14. How did your greenside approach change?

15. How did you adjust after the first shot?

After you've completed this initial assessment, it's time to move on to the lesson goal-setting, benchmarking and lesson-planning segments of Real Golf. We're going to dive into those next.

NOTES

CHAPTER 3

Goal-Setting and Benchmarking

"What gets measured gets improved."

You have some basic analysis of your game's strengths and weaknesses down on paper, and you've played a Real Golf self-scramble.

Now what?

How do you use that framework to improve your game, and how do you measure your progress?

One of the basic tenets of management consulting is that what gets measured gets improved. The first step in any consulting relationship is for the consultant to immerse himself or herself in the organization's operations and culture and determine which aspects of the business are the most important. Then, it's a matter of creating metrics to measure those aspects of the business.

That's obviously a simplification, but for the purposes of golf instruction it works extremely well. Our goal here is to help you find a series of simple, well-defined "measurables," in your game and use the self-scramble technique to track and improve those measurables. When you improve those measurables, your scores will inevitably go down. And by focusing on measurables—the process part of the game—you're deflecting your attention from outcome, the place where emotions often get the better of you.

To use a bad biz-speak cliché, it's win-win.

When I work with my students in person, I start by breaking down the game into specific skill areas:

Tee shots

Full swing shots from fairway and rough

Off-speed approach shots/pitches

Short game shots around the green

Bunker around the green

Putting

Course strategy

Emotional management

I'll start with a simple question for you. Using the results of your assessment and first self-scramble, which ONE of these areas would you pick as the one you'd most like to improve?

Let's say it's tee shots. What specifically do you think is your problem? Do you need more power? Do you struggle with accuracy? Do you have trouble making consistent contact?

By far the most common comment I get when I ask this question is some variation of "I want to be more consistent." That's an understandable complaint, but it requires some more digging before we get to our "measurable."

When you play your regular game, how many penalty shots do you average per round? My definition includes both actual penalty shots that come from hitting out of bounds or into a hazard and punch-out shots you hit just to get back into play. Is it four? Ten?

Now compare that number to a common one like "fairways hit." It seems intuitive to believe that hitting six fairways in a round is better than hitting four, and it might be on a given day. But I don't think fairways hit is a precise enough measurement for most players. Unless you're playing courses with extremely penal rough, you could well be in better shape 250 yards down the hole and in the light first cut than 200 yards down in the middle of the fairway. I'd rather you keep track of your tee shots in terms of "in-play" and "out-of-play."

Here's what I mean. The first hole at the Glen Club is a 540-yard par-5. There's a bunker that starts about 220 yards down, on the left side of the fairway. Let's say you decide to aim at the bunker and play for your standard 10-yard fade. You make your swing and look up, expecting to see that curve, but the ball goes on a rope, straight toward that bunker. When you get to the ball, you see that you really caught it, and it carried the bunker into the light rough on the other side. You have a perfect line on your second shot, and a much shorter club in your hand. In Real Golf terms, that's a win.

Some extremely smart people have crunched a lot of numbers and figured out what the "safest" plays are in terms of tee shot strategy. You can use the benefit of that research to start informing some of the decisions you make off the tee. Mark Broadie of Columbia University figured out that 10-handicappers who aim straight down the middle of the fairway hit a shot out of bounds about 8 percent of the time. Twenty-handicappers hit OB about 15 percent of the time aiming straight. Adjust the aiming point to the edge of the left rough and the 10-handicapper's OB percentage drops to 1.5 percent—and the 20-handicapper's drops to about the same!

This is just the most basic data from Mark's research, but it absolutely proves my point. If you start measuring your drives as in play and out of play and start aiming away from the biggest trouble spots, you have the opportunity to shave at least four shots off your handicap—without changing a single thing about your swing.

Instead of looking at the pie-in-the-sky PGA Tour fairways hit stats—where world class players hit about 10 of 14 every round—start making it your goal to hit every tee shot in play, where you can advance the second shot toward the target.

One of my favorite new statistics on the PGA Tour is "strokes gained"—which measures how a given player performs relative to what the entire rest of the field did on a given day. A few years ago, I had Golf Digest Top 50 teacher Hank Haney come to Chicago to do a full-day Ultimate Scoring School with me for the Chicago District Golf Association. Hank's take on strokes gained is extremely perceptive—and extremely appropriate for the average amateur.

In slicing and dicing the statistics during his work with Tiger Woods, Hank determined that the three areas that produce the most "strokes lost" to the field are three-putts, penalty shots and bad short game shots that needed two chips to get on the green.

You can create your own personalized "strokes gained" measurement by determining how many penalty shots you take in a round, how many times you three-putt, and how many times you can't get down in three shots from around the green—a chip and two putts, max.

Those simple barometers are going to tell you a huge amount about your game, and where you need to focus your work to improve.

The beauty of the Real Golf self-scramble is that you can record your stats for ALL of the shots you hit throughout the experiment. As you can imagine, you have the opportunity to build up a substantial amount of information in a relatively short period of time. Here are just a few of the measurements you can try:

-Tee shots in play
-Tee shot penalties

-Greens hit

-Penalty shots on approaches

-Short game attempts

-Short game conversions (up and down)

-Sand shot attempts

-Average distance after sand shot

-Sand shot conversions (up and down)

-One-putt greens

-Two-putt greens

-Estimated length of first putt

-Estimated length of second putt

The blizzard of data can certainly overwhelm you if you let it. That's why I recommend starting with a single skill area and keeping stats on that are first before moving on to the next one.

As far as recording stats, you can be as high-tech or low-tech as you prefer. Segmenting a standard scorecard into little boxes and keeping notes there worked for Johnny Miller, and he was only one of the greatest ball-strikers of all-time. At RealGolfBook.com, you can find free sample scorecards to download and print. They're already pre-formatted to measure some of the stats we've talked about here. You can also use one of the many score- and stat-tracking apps that have been developed for smart phones. The obvious advantage there is that the app automatically accumulates the data and shows you your trends.

The second piece of the data puzzle is benchmarking your game against your goals. It's great to show improvement in any of these areas, but how do you know how much more road there is to travel to reach the next level of proficiency? Consultants compare the measurable of one organization to an index of similar measureables from companies in the same business. You can do the same.

Take the greens in regulation stat, for example. Tour players hit around 13 greens per round. A 20-handicapper might hit two. A good rule of thumb is that every additional green you hit over your average usually results in about a shot and half improvement on your scorecard.

Reducing three putts is the lowest hanging fruit for any player. A 20-handicapper averages anywhere from two to five three-putts per round. Some slight improvement in short game technique—more putting opportunities closer to the hole—and improved speed control can virtually eliminate three-putting except on the most challenging greens.

For more information on applicable benchmarks, Dr. Lucius Riccio's article in the May 2008 issue of Golf Digest provides a fascinating snapshot on how players of different handicaps reach their scores. Check it out on GolfDigest.com.

NOTES

CHAPTER 4

Playing Lesson Formats and Strategies

"Troubleshoot your game and work on solutions in the environment in which you're going to play for real."

After you've completed **your game** assessment and preliminary round of Real Golf, you're in position to make real changes to your game. The traditional way to do that has been to take a bunch of lessons on the range, and hit buckets and buckets of balls with the hope that the skills you learn there eventually translate to the course.

I want to stress again that the Real Golf plan doesn't discount the value of traditional golf instruction. And I'm not trying to get you to break up with your teacher. My goal is to get you to troubleshoot your game and work on solutions in the environment in which you're going to play for real. Everything about the range is deceptive. There are no real consequences for hitting bad shots, and you're tempted to start firing balls out like they're on an assembly line. The rhythm feels good at the time, but it isn't helping you get better at the real thing—even when you're getting some affirmation from your pro.

Try this instead. Approach your next Real Golf round as a "golf scrimmage." Just like the basketball or football scrimmages you might have played in as a high-schooler, a scrimmage is a practice held under real game conditions.

One of my favorite "next-level" learn-as-you play routines doesn't even require a full 9- or 18-hole round. You can do it on a circuit of three or four holes at your course, and it gives your complete game—from the mind to shot execution—a workout.

On your first tee, take 60 seconds to visualize what your "par" score for the hole would be, and exactly how you would achieve it. I'm not talking about visualizing a 320-yard tee shot and a 5-iron to two feet for a tap-in birdie. If you're playing a 400-yard par-4 as a 20-handicapper, it might mean visualizing a tee shot, an approach 30 or 40 yards short of the hole, a pitch and two putts. Bogey is a good "par" score for you. The point is to visualize what you're going to execute for an acceptable result.

Now, play that hole with one ball. If you end up matching your visualized score, proceed to the next hole and repeat the exercise. But if your actual score ends up higher than the "par" score you visualized on the tee, go to the next hole and change up the drill.

Start the same way, by visualizing yourself executing whatever your personal par is for that next hole, shot by shot. Instead of playing one ball, give yourself a second opportunity at a shot—but only if you need it. For example, if you hit a decent tee shot, go ahead and move to your approach. If you catch that one a little thin, hit another from the same spot and pick the best one. The objective is to make the most out of your extra shots—but to use as few of them as possible.

You can set the bar wherever you like for a three- or four-hole circuit. But obviously the goal is to reduce to zero the number of extra shots you use to produce your "par" score.

The cool thing about this exercise is that you will soon find yourself swinging more freely—and you'll start to record hole results that are actually better than your personal par. That's the sign of real improvement in your game.

To dial in more finely on a particular area of your overall game to improve, you can modify the self-scramble game to suit that goal. Say you want to improve your tee shots. You can adapt the three-ball scramble to be "in-play" for three tee balls, but then you play the best one of those into the hole one shot at a time. The same would hold true for approaches or putts—one shot at a time around the course until you get to those chances, where you would then get three.

One of the more popular self-scramble programs my top-tier juniors use centers on the short game. They'll play with one ball for all of the other shots around the course, but use the three-ball technique for one aspect of the short game during a given round. One day, it might be greenside bunker shots, while another day it could be chip shots. It makes for fantastic practice under real course conditions, both because you're getting actual reps of the shots in, and because you're reading the shot and seeing the trajectory and roll in real life. It doesn't take long for an area of weakness to become an area of strength.

Putting is also a natural place for self-scramble. Whether you use it for all of your first putts, to improve your read and speed, or for all putts—to see more balls go in the hole—it's better than any kind of practice you could do on the putting green up by the clubhouse. This strategy is not much different than the one tour players use during practice rounds before a professional event. You'll see players drop a few balls around the green to hit practice putts to places where they know they'll be seeing pin locations during the tournament. They're scrimmaging for the tournament round to come.

Will hitting three balls magically cure a severe mechanical problem? Not by itself. But it will encourage you to become more attuned to what you're doing, and give you more feedback to share with your swing coach. You can then intersperse your on-course scrimmages with some fine-tuning at the practice tee to address any ongoing mechanical issues. It's even more productive to go out and play one of these three- or four-hole mini-scrimmages with your coach and get that feedback as the game is happening.

Most players don't pay nearly enough attention to the strategic aspect of the game. The reality is that you can probably score much better—at least five shots better if you're an 18-handicapper—just by making better decisions. And that's without making a single change to your mechanics.

The self-scramble format is fantastic for this kind of work. For example, take that short 300-yard par-4 at your course. Maybe it has trouble on one side, or deep bunkers protecting the green. You can use the three-ball scramble to play it with different strategies to assess the best one to pick when it's for real. Use your driver and try to get down close to the hole, and then hit a hybrid and play it safe. Play it out when you miss into those deep bunkers and find out just how realistic an up and down is. If the shot isn't as scary as you thought, it reduces the stress on you the next time you're facing that approach shot. You've lost that fear of the unknown.

After a handful of strategic self-scrambles around your course, you will have built a pretty good road map of each hole's ideal path. You won't always hit the best shot or stay on the path, but your odds for success are much better when you have a positive plan—not a reactive one.

I'm sure you can see what the next logical step is in the process. Once you're consistently recording scores of par or better with the three-ball technique, it's time to take the next step and limit yourself to two balls per shot. You're dialing up the pressure—something every player needs to proof his or her game–but you still have that margin of forgiveness to learn from a mistake and make it right.

When my college-bound players have gotten to a plateau with the two-ball technique, we move to what I call one-ball-plus. In this game, you start out with 18 extra shots you can use at any time on the course—even if you want to take two or three repeat shots after a single mishit. Your goal is to finish the round using no more than that allocation of 18 extra shots.

Depending on your level of progression, you can then shave one extra shot from that buffer on each subsequent practice round— staying at the previous level until you've completed it successfully.

Let me give you one real-world case study of this process so you can get a feel for how quickly results can come. One of my female high school players started playing in regional AJGA events before her junior year. She has a great swing, but it wasn't translating into the scores she expected. She was shooting in the 90s, when she expected to be in the low 80s.

She started the Real Golf scrimmage plan the same way you've read here—with nine holes of three-ball self-scramble. She shot 3-under, and said it immediately helped her realize that she had the swing and the talent to record those kinds of scores. After a month of mixing in several of the different games we've been talking about here, she decided to play 18 holes using the three-ball scramble. She called me afterward just overjoyed about shooting a 6-under 66.

After shooting near par in both the two-ball and 18-shot scramble games, she was ready for the high school season. By the end of the fall, she was team MVP and an all-conference selection, and she won the individual conference tournament with a round of 77. Playing in her final high school golf season, with the pressure of the conference, regional, sectional and state high school final tournament on the line, she shot rounds of 77-78-75-80-83-74 to lead New Trier to a fourth place finish overall in Illinois HS Golf.

Now, she's getting ready for the very real possibility of playing college golf.

The key? Real Golf self-scrambling gave her the immediate sense that she could "go low," and record scores much lower than she had been comfortable shooting. In tournament situations, she would play the first five or six holes at even par or 1-over and be able to tell herself that she'd been there before. She knew the feeling and it wasn't surprising or uncomfortable.

And it all came from practicing like she played.

BONUS

"Build on the Real Golf scrimmage system with a series of mental and physical training exercises that will help you develop a complete game."

There's no question that **following** the simple Real Golf prescription I've described here will make you a better golfer in as little as 30 days—enough time to play a few scrimmage circuits.

Where you go from there—and how good you want to be—is up to you. You can use this Real Golf mini-program just like you would a set of fitness DVDs, and go back through the program multiple times. You'll certainly get a benefit out of it.

But to really become the best player you can be, you're going to want to build on the Real Golf scrimmage system with a series of physical and mental training exercises that will help you develop a complete game.

I'd like to give you a preview of those programs, which you'll be able to find in the coming editions of Real Golf.

The best kind of physical and mechanical training for golf gives you the opportunity to make the most out of your location. It's obviously great to be able to use the range whenever you like, but the reality for most people is that work, family and weather get in the way.

Here are three drills to get you started.

Club Head Through Handle Connection

Objective: Increase awareness, touch, feel and image of the most critical connection between your swing, your clubs and your golf ball.

Pick a middle iron from your bag. Sit in a chair and take your normal grip. Spend 60 seconds examining your hands while lightly tightening and loosening your grip. Extend and retract your arms, feeling the muscles in your arms and hands move in relation to each other.

Now extend your arms as if somebody is pulling on the clubhead. Check to make sure that in this position, the leading edge of the clubhead is square, not open or closed. If it's open or closed, adjust your grip accordingly so that the leading edge is square when your arms are extended.

From the same seated position, flip the club around and hold it by the head, in two hands. Close your eyes, and use your hands and fingers to feel the contours of the head. Now, using only your sense of touch, maneuver your hands down the shaft and take your grip. The goal is to set your grip perfectly—with the leading edge of the clubhead square, as in the first part of the drill—using only feel, not sight. After you set your grip, open your eyes to see if your vision backs up what you feel. Adjust if necessary and repeat the exercise. Do this for each club in your bag once a day and you'll make tremendous strides in your feel for the club and the clubhead.

Mirror Swing Building

Objective: Get a more accurate sense of

what your swing actually looks like—not just how it feels.

Set up in front of a mirror in a room with high enough ceilings and enough empty space so that you can swing a club freely. If you're on a hard floor, use a piece of astroturf or carpet so that you can brush the ground with your club.

With a 9-iron or wedge, take your address position—keeping your feet set about a foot apart from instep to instep. Set your club in the middle of your stance, with a ball just ahead of it. Spend 60 seconds in your setup position, but with your head slightly raised so you can look into the mirror. Once you're happy with your setup and balance, close your eyes and return your head to your normal setup position. Hold this position for 20 seconds, then open your eyes and re-check your position.

Now, straighten and hold the club in your dominant hand only, resting on the ground. Close your eyes and get back into your setup position using only feel. Once you're there, open your eyes to check to see if it matches your feel.

If it does, make a turn so that the mirror is off of your left side (right side for left-handed players). Go through this same process again, checking yourself from the down-the-line angle.

Return to the face-on position and get into your setup with your eyes closed—this time with no ball in place. Once you've checked and are happy with your position, close your eyes again and make some very slow swings, brushing the ground in front of you lightly. Swing at 25 or 30 percent speed, feeling for the brush of the ground. Now open your eyes and repeat this drill at the same speed.

The goal here is not to work on the technical aspects of the swing, but to feel the connection between your body and the club. Increase the speed of the drill slowly until you're at about 75 percent speed. Try to make consistent contact with the ground at the same spot each time.

Mental training is just as important as physical training, and one of my favorite techniques in that area is something I call the Human Highlight Shot Reel. To try it, sit back in your favorite chair and close your eyes. Starting with the driver, think back to your favorite on-course moments with each club. It could be a situational memory, like a great drive in a big spot, or it could simply be a time when you hit the longest or best shot of your life. For each shot, think about the details with as much color as you can. Where were you? What course? What hole? Can you actually see the trajectory of the ball, and what it does when it lands? How did you feel right after the shot? What did your playing partners say about it?

For each club and each shot you

remember, jot down a few notes on a piece of paper—a kind of great shot shorthand. You don't need to go into the full description. Just something that will remind you when you see it again.

Once you have your list, use it the next time you complete this technique. Each time, try to go deeper and deeper into your memory banks. For a great iron shot on a par-3, can you remember walking onto the tee box and putting your tee into the ground? Do you remember where the tee markers were, and what the wind was doing?

You might not have many details when you start this process, but you'll be surprised at how much color returns as you do it again and again. Your mind will recognize some emerging memories of these great shots and provide you with details you thought were gone.

This collection of shorthand highlight notes is one of the most valuable tools you can have for your mental game. It's a powerful way to help you both learn the art of visualizing and develop the skill of pre-programming your mind with positive outcomes. As you get better at it, you'll get more and more control over that skill. The best players can stand over an important shot and actually access those positive memories about some other shot they've already hit with that club. Then the goal becomes copying that feel for this one—which is a powerful and positive use of your mind at a time when it's easy to be distracted by pressure and negative thoughts.

At RealGolfBook.com, you can share your own inspirational scoring stories, read stories from others, and download all the scorecards and tools you need to play your best golf!

Bosco Box Breathing

Or, as my state championship high school team called it, B-Cubed. This process helps improve your focus, coordination and decision-making. The research behind it comes from the fine folks at HeartMath.

Sit comfortably and close your eyes. Breathe in, and then exhale continuously until you have emptied your lungs. Hold for a slow count of four, and then inhale as deeply as you can through your nose, until your lungs are full. Hold this for a slow count of four, and then exhale through your mouth, as if you're blowing out a candle a foot away. Empty your lungs completely.

Continue this cycle nine or more times. I visualize a picture frame as I'm doing it— starting at one side for the exhale, the bottom as the hold, the other side as the inhale, and the top as another hold. Within that frame can be whatever mental image provides calmness or confidence for you—anything that makes you happy! I'll picture on my kids' faces, or even a favorite desert.

I really want to hear from you about your own Joe Bosco Real Golf experiences!

Whether its by email, or through my Realgolfbook.com or Joeboscogolf.com websites.

To schedule a Real Golf lesson or create a customized special Real Golf Event at your club or organization, please call 1-855-JOE-GOLF or send me an email at joeboscogolf@gmail.com.

NOTES

ACKNOWLEDGEMENTS

So many people have **influenced** me directly or indirectly in the creating of this book. Saying thank you and letting people past and present know that they have had an impact on my and my life's work is a lump-in-the-throat experience. I am blessed to do what I do and with the people I do it with and for.

For my family: Mary, Isabella & Julia Bosco; Barbara Fasano, Ronald Bosco, Carla & Mike Dainko; Maria, Stephen, John & Anne Baird; Anne Fasano, Paul Jiganti, Jack Jiganti, Raymond & Dorothy Tasch; Julie Tasch & Ed Agasi; Chuck, Sandy, Nick & Will Tasch; Donna, Fred, and Joe, Michael & Matthew Plecha.

To friends, mentors and past and present students: Paul Jiganti, Barry Cronin; Sam, Honey & William Skinner, Eric Mogentale, Scott Murray, Vernon Loucks, Steve Lesnik, Josh Lesnik, Steve Skinner, Gary Binder, Greg Noack, Bob Mack, John Preschlack, Richard & Rebecca Halpern, Annika Welander, Helge Fischer, Jack Jiganti, Paul Sheridan, Sheila Hansen, Stan Utley, Mike Adams, Rudy Duran, Hank Haney, Dick Wagley, Emil Esposito, E.A. Tischler, Sara Dickson, Tim Leahy, Andrew Louthain, Ernie Roth, Al Lerner, Bobby Foster, Jim Bodman, Peter Donahue, Mark Donahue, Dr. Jim Payne, Jeff Quicksilver, Tony Lapasso, Art and Michael Slaven, Brian, Coleen, April, Jenny, Maggie & Mary Gelber, Charlie Besser, Jim Boedecker, Peter Russell, James Malles, James Kaplan, Ed Gubam, Dean Teglia, Bill Lenz, Steve Murray, Pat, Melinda, Connor & Luke Baldwin, Bill, Carolyn, & Michael Kinsella, Richard, Lauri, Lexi, Liza & Zachary Salberg, Steve Kisslinger, Jon Denham, Kevin Krantz, Eric Freidler, Chris Inglot, Jerry Maatman, Debbie Radakovich, Mike & Angie Berman, Ken & Kelly Kennerly, Matt &

Nicholas McCall, Terry Duffy, Karen Perlman, Jason Sacks, Scott & Thomas Shimamoto, Ian & Lauren Kelsey, Josh Johnson, Jim Weinburg, Ryan Kowalski, Patrick McHugh, Jay Bach, Michael, David & Andrew Blechman, Ron Rolighed, Keith Olson; John, Clint & Douglas Mabie, Bret Schoch, Jacqueline Wacker, Carrie Williams, Stephanie Schwartz, John & Melissa Kenny, Peggy Schweller; Larry, Denise, Robert & Emily Fisher; Eric, Felisse, Andrew & Lauren Sigurdson, Chris & Rebecca Lindblad, George & Sean Furman, Matt Jones, Suzanne Lynch, Hillary Leisten, Dan Maguire, Seulki Park, Sara Dickson, Tony Persico, Scott Gajdel, Joe Johnson, Nick Becks, John Louis, Emma & John Vickery, Brandon Nasitir, Wayne Arner, Liz Kohler, Ken Lieberman, Lewis Kaplan, Jackie Schropshire, Bill Moeller, Ben Loss, George Emme, Matthew Tritley, Garrett Muscatel, Rick Schuham, Dale Thomas, Pam Belter, Rachel Rhee, Mike McQuillen, Dana Hayes & Dana Hayes Jr., Greg & Luke Gibson, Walt & Michael Bay, David Limardi, John Fern, Al Stonich, Andy & Martha Hick, Steve Kisslinger, Tom Walker, Tommy Tech McHugh, Ed Tindall, Rob Mathias, Bob Vorwald, Roger Boehm, Bill Blackwell, Don Crowe, Peter Kanaris, Steve Sacks & Heather Ludington, Phil Arouca, Dave Crowell, Will Dron, Tom Filippini, Annika Welander, Craig Whitehead, Ed Gubman, Emily Senko, Julianne McInerney, Jim Nugent, Robert Marcioni and Suzanne Crawford Dennis.

Special thanks to Kemper Sports and the management and staff of The Glen Club in Glenview IL, and to the North Shore Country Day School Administration, Staff, Athletic department, team members and families.

Positive Coaching Alliance

My teaching philosophy is anchored by the premise that you get what you think, so you should think positively. If you take a playing lesson from me at the Glen Club, attend one of my clinics or workshops, or use the tactics in this book, the central skill you're developing is the belief that you can improve.

It's about being—and staying—positive.

As I was developing the Real Golf approach to learning, I was introduced to a national organization that resonated deeply with me—The Positive Coaching Alliance (PCA). The PCA's mission is to transform the culture of youth sports so that young athletes can have a positive, character-building experience. Its National Advisory Board is a who's who of professional and college sports—Phil Jackson, Tony LaRussa and Dean Smith are just a few on that list.

In 2013, I was invited to join the PCA's Chicago Chapter Board of Directors. I believe it is one of the noblest causes in youth athletics.

Below, you'll find a description of what the PCA is all about. Please consider volunteering to help your local or regional group.

Positive Coaching Alliance

Positive Coaching Alliance (PCA) is a national non-profit organization with the mission to transform the culture of youth sports so that youth athletes can have a positive, character-building experience. PCA achieves its goals primarily by providing training workshops to coaches, parents, and administrators of schools and youth sports organizations in the United States. Founded in 1998, PCA has conducted more than 10,000 workshops for more than 1,700 schools and youth sports organizations, affecting more than 4.5 million youth and high school athletes.[1] PCA Founder and Executive Director Jim Thompson launched PCA in 1998 within the Stanford University Athletic Department after seeing a "win-at-all-cost" mentality in youth sports while coaching his son's baseball team. Positive Coaching Alliance was created with the mission to "transform youth sports so sports can transform youth." Its mission statement has since been modified to "Better Athletes, Better People."

Mission

"Better Athletes, Better People"

PCA's philosophy focuses on sports as an opportunity for character education, espousing the Double-Goal Coach, whose first goal is winning, and whose second, more important goal is teaching life lessons through sports.

Positive Coaching Alliance has three national goals:

1. Replace "win-at-all-cost" coaching with Double-Goal Coaching

2. Help youth sports organization leaders create a culture in which "Honoring the Game" is the norm

3. Spark and fuel a "social epidemic" of Positive Coaching in the United States

Philosophy

Positive Coaching Alliance developed "The Positive Coaching Mental Model", a research summary based upon several psychological studies, in order to guide youth sports coaches in creating positive and effective team cultures. The model comprises three principles:

-Redefining "Winner"

Focusing on mastery of skill, rather than on scoreboard results, decreases anxiety and gives youth athletes a sense of control over the outcome. Positive Coaches recognize that mistakes are an inevitable part of sports and cultivate effort rather than concern about outcome, fostering an environment in which players don't fear making mistakes.

-Filling "Emotional Tanks"

Positive Coaches frequently give truthful, specific praise, laying the groundwork for "teachable moments," when players will be receptive to specific, constructive criticism.

-Honoring the Game

Positive Coaches train their athletes to respect Rules, Opponents, Officials, Teammates, and Self (R.O.O.T.S.)

For more information, please visit the Positive Coaching Alliance website at http://www.positivecoach.org.

A portion of the proceeds from the sale of this book go to the Positive Coaching Alliance.

Trusted Resources

MentalGolfWorkshopProfile.com

To get a great snapshot of your mental game, try the assessment at Bobby Foster's MentalGolfWorkshopProfile.com. Use the promotional code BOSCO, or go to RealGolfBook.com and click on the MentalGolfProfile link.

Big Moss Golf

To keep your game sharp at home, a putting green is a great investment. Big Moss Golf's low-cast surfaces are fantastic. Use the promotional code REAL GOLF at www.bigmossgolf.com for a special discount.

Edel Golf

My friends at Edel not only make some of the most finely crafted putters and wedges you can buy. They also have the most comprehensive fitting system in the game. By adjusting head design, lie angle, length, loft, hosel design, offset, aiming line placement, shaft flex and swing weight, Edel's master fitters find the ideal prescription from more than 300 million build combinations. Each putter is literally a one-off, custom-built work of engineering art for one specific person—you.

Edel's wedges are just as special. Golf Digest Top 50 teacher Mike Adams—one of Edel Golf's co-founders—worked with David Edel to create a series of wedges that provide all players with the advantages of a tour wedge fitting experience. By measuring angle of attack and shaft lean at impact, players are fit into one of eight grinds with bounce angles ranging from eight to 22 degrees. By minimizing the club's resistance to digging, Edel wedges help players begin to lose their fear of hitting shots fat and thin. Fifteen different shaft options ensure that you'll have optimal launch conditions, spin rates, and distance consistency. And with wedges ranging from 46 to 64 in one degree increments, the Edel wedge system has your complete short game needs covered.

Go to EdelGolf.com to find a regional fitter near you, or contact Matt Jones at mjones@edelgolf.com for fittings in the Illinois-Wisconsin-Northern Missouri region.